DOCUMENTING MY JOURNEY UNCOVER UNHEEDED REALITIES

EVERYONE HAS A STORY OF THEIR OWN STRUGGLE; LET'S CHANGE THE CLIMAX NOW.

AASHI SHARMA

I dedicate this book to my family and some mentors. Their unwavering support and inspiration have guided me through every chapter of this journey. Your belief in me made this exploration possible. May it inspire others to embark on their own path of uncovering truths. This book is also dedicated to anyone who dares to question and seek deeper truths.

Contents

Foreword — *vii*

Preface — *ix*

Acknowledgements — *xi*

Prologue — *xiii*

1. This Part Of My Life Is Called "Timid And Taunted" — 1

2. Don't Be So Hard On Yourself — 4

3. Regret Sucks! — 8

4. You Are The Main Character Of Your Life — 20

5. The Game Of "Why Not?" — 25

6. A Stem Of Fear "Comfort Zone" — 32

7. "Mindset" — 46

8. True Happiness? Zero Expectation — 50

9. Explore The Power Of Exploration — 53

10. Try & Taste Everything — 55

11. This Part Of My Life, This Little Part Of My Life Called "Happiness" — 56

Epilogue — 59

Foreword

Life is a maze of challenges, turning points, and hidden truths. *Documenting My Journey Uncover Unheeded Realities*, invites you into a deeply personal exploration of these complexities.

In this book, you'll follow my path through the twists of doubt, moments of realization, and transformative change. It's a candid look at the highs and lows that shape our lives and the resilience we discover along the way. The climax isn't a grand revelation but the ongoing journey of seeking and understanding. It's in those everyday moments of clarity and struggle where the real story unfolds. What you hold in your hands is not just a record of your experiences but a reflection on the universal quest for understanding and growth. Aashi aims to illuminate the process of self-discovery by telling the truth, showing that we are all superheroes and have a special strength inside us that can transform our lives. Within these pages, I hope you will find connections to your own experiences and gain insights that resonate with your path. Thank you for being part of this journey. Your involvement adds meaning and makes it all worthwhile.

Preface

As I write the preface to *"Documenting My Journey Uncover Unheeded Realities,"* I aim to share the insights and truths from my ordinary life. I am privileged to reveal these parts of my journey to show that nothing is impossible if you have carried a courageous soul within you.

This is about our universal struggle to understand ourselves and our place in the world, embracing the process of self-discovery and the revelations along the way. So, let's embark on this journey together. Readers, your engagement brings life to every word and turns every page. Your enthusiasm makes all the difference.

Acknowledgements

As I reflect on the journey that brought this book to life, I am overwhelmed with gratitude for the incredible people who have supported me along the way.

First and foremost, my deepest thanks go to my family. Your unwavering support and boundless belief in my dreams have been the bedrock of this endeavor. Through every late-night writing session and moments of doubt, your encouragement and love have been my greatest strength. You've been my cheerleaders and my anchors, and for that, I am profoundly grateful.

To my mentors, you have been the guiding lights in this labyrinth of creativity. Your wisdom, patience, and constructive feedback have shaped my growth as a writer. Each piece of advice, every insightful critique, and your steadfast belief in my potential have illuminated my path, helping me navigate the challenges of this journey. Your influence is deeply woven into the fabric of this book.

A heartfelt thank you to my online readers. Your engagement with my work has been both inspiring and humbling. The thoughtful comments, constructive corrections, and words of encouragement you've shared have not only sharpened my writing but have also ignited my passion. Each interaction has been a lesson, and every suggestion has been a stepping stone toward improvement. Your support has been a vital part of this journey, and I cherish the connection we've built through our shared love of storytelling.

Together, you have all played an integral role in this exploration of truth and self-discovery. This book is as much a testament to your support as it is to my own efforts. Thank you for being part of this adventure and for helping bring *"Documenting My Journey Uncover Unheeded Realities"* to life.

Prologue

In India, many parents dream of their children becoming engineers, doctors, or securing government jobs. These professions are viewed as the golden tickets to a secure and stable future. The promise of financial security and need to meet societal expectations often overshadow other career paths.

However, not everyone is suited for these roles. Some people are naturally inclined toward careers like art, design, or writing, and may find true fulfilment in these fields. Yet, many parents push their children towards traditional roles, even if those paths don't align with their passions or skills.

When you truly love what you do, work becomes effortless, and you're driven by passion, not just money. Unfortunately, societal expectations can trap people in careers they don't enjoy, making them feel like failures if they don't meet those expectations.

The pressure to conform starts early, with education often focusing more on grades than personal growth. My parents wanted me to succeed and encouraged me to prepare for government exams, but this path didn't align with my true desires. Their intentions were rooted in love, but it's crucial to recognize that true success lies in following one's own passions.

Imagine a world where children are encouraged to pursue what truly excites them, without fear of judgment. Success is about personal fulfilment, not just meeting societal expectations.

CHAPTER ONE

This Part Of My Life is Called "Timid and Taunted"

I want to take you from the real world to the inner world. If you truly want something, you've got to work for it. Whether it's your first love or your dream job, no one will hand it to you on a silver platter. You have to earn it, whether it takes a day, two months, or ten years. Not everything is just about winning; something is worth fighting for. It's about fighting for it and making it yours.

After graduating high school, I was surrounded by people asking the same questions, "What's your passion? What's your dream? Where do you envision yourself in the next five years?" One thing that cleared my mind since school was that I would become a proficient lecturer. How? Well, I was figuring it out.

Anyway, I soon quickly realised that to become a lecturer, I needed to focus on two key areas: Building confidence and enhancing communication. It was clear that improving my communication skills was crucial to achieving my goal because of two reasons. First, I had a timid nature and low self-esteem. Second, becoming a professor demands overcoming these two challenges.

Everyone around me seemed to know but never suggested was this—if you're weak at something, find a reason why and a way to turn that weakness into a strength. But, because of my shy nature, I struggled to articulate my thoughts and could never muster the courage to say "no" to anyone.

People who can't protect themselves, lose everything that they have, I believe in that. I often hesitated and doubted my abilities, hinting at a lack of self-awareness. Deep down, a curious part of me wanted to speak up but couldn't, from but into two things held me back: The fear of losing those I cared about and not wanted to hurt anyone's feelings. It created a timid image of me in the minds of those around me.

But then, it all started to make sense. I couldn't wait for the next chapter to begin. So, I enrolled in a nearby Personality Development and English Speaking course. On the first day, I was pumped and ready to dive into something new today.

I sat in the last row among fifty students, feeling incredibly shy and uncertain. The room hummed as everyone anticipated what the day's class would bring. Suddenly, the chatter ceased as a tall figure entered—dressed sharply in a formal shirt, black pants, and polished shoes. It was clear from his commanding presence that he was a seasoned instructor and well-respected in this place. His confidence and charisma immediately captivated the room, and all eyes turned to him as he took his place at the podium.

"Good morning, everyone!" His voice rang out with enthusiasm, instantly grabbing our attention. He introduced himself as our instructor, his genuine warmth forming a welcoming tone for the class. But what truly set him apart was his unique approach to teaching. He made ordinary concepts exciting through songs, drama, writing exercises, and even acting, turning every lesson into an engaging and enlightening experience. That's the mere reason everybody wanted to take his class.

Before wrapping up, he assigned us our first task: in the next session, all of us would introduce ourselves at the podium. It seemed simple, but for someone like me, it was nerve-wracking. Trying something new is always intimidating. It wasn't a big deal, but I was still worried about the outcome. Unfortunately, I fell ill and couldn't prepare for the next day. Unexpectedly, something worse happened that I hadn't anticipated.

As he called each student to the podium, my anxiety grew with every name he read. When it was finally my turn, I stood before fifty classmates, their eyes on me. I tried to begin with, "Hello everyone, I'm Aashi Sharma," but my voice faltered and trailed off. The confidence I had worked so hard to build seemed to vanish instantly. My hands shook, and I couldn't look anyone in the eye. Feeling overwhelmed, I looked down and struggled to get my words out.

As I gathered the courage to speak up, my voice trembled and my cheeks flushed, but before I could continue, he abruptly interrupted me in his harsh tone and unrelenting. "Without practice, what are you doing here?" The impact of his words felt like a punch, and tears started to form in my eyes. He told me in front of the class, "You'll never learn anything in life." I stood there, stunned and embarrassed. I was the type of person who easily got upset and cried when others criticize me. I didn't feel good. I tried to explain my situation, but he just brushed it off as an excuse.

It's hard to find courage when you feel immature and uncertain.

Six months later, I did everything to prove I was serious about learning something important. So, I attended extra classes, actively joined in various activities, and practiced communicating regularly, whether in front of the mirror or with others and finally, the moment came around. Among many students, he selected three students from his four batches for the prestigious platform "Success Gyan." Guess what? I was one of them.

Real Talk: No matter how many times you stumble, it's up to you to get back up. Only you know what you truly want and what you're capable of. Don't depend on others to fix things for you or make you feel better. Eventually, things will come together. Rest assured, everything will inevitably align in your favor.

CHAPTER TWO

Don't Be So Hard On Yourself

As the results for the twelfth class were about to be announced, I felt a mix of excitement and tension gripping me; I had previously made it clear to my parents that I wanted to pursue English Honors to achieve my goal.I felt a mix of excitement and tension gripping me; I had previously made it clear to my parents that I wanted to pursue English Honors to achieve my goal. I needed to secure high marks in order to get admission to the best college.

On the day of the English exam, I entered the room confidently. Being too excited and overconfident led me to make a huge mistake. Instead of using the right method of doing each question carefully in less time, especially on long questions, I took 30 minutes for each one.

I had prepared thoroughly to get into the best college for English Honors at Delhi University. But at that moment, all my plans seemed to crumble. I left the exam hall feeling disappointed, knowing I had let my excitement get the better of me. Here's a plot twist:

It's natural to feel unfortunate when things go in the opposite direction. My confidence and courage took a hit. I scored above the 60s and 70s in other subjects, but in English, where I had hoped to shine, I got just 49. It was a mark I had never imagined I'd get especially, in my favourite subject. Ironically, I scored 92 in

Geography, a subject I didn't need. Those numbers felt meaningless to me. God was testing my efforts, patience, and self-belief.

If I had managed my time better, I would have been happier. Instead, I was left blaming myself and carrying a pain I couldn't explain to anyone. Everyone had advice, but no one understood how much that English mark meant to me.

With no other choice or interest, I decided to take an improvement exam the following year. In the meantime, I enrolled in a B.A. program with zero interest, biding my time until I could retake my English exam. I practiced diligently to manage my time effectively. Eventually, I dropped out in the second year of college after achieving 81% in English.

But that wasn't the end of it. The following year, university cutoffs soared higher than ever before, and I missed out on admission to the colleges I had hoped for. With no other options left, I pursued my career through an open university, ensuring I wouldn't regret my decision later on. Looking back, I learned preparation and confidence are crucial, as are managing your time and emotions. It was a setback, but it taught me the importance of staying calm and focused, regardless of how prepared or excited I might be.

Start Owning Your Shit

That journey taught me more than just academics; it taught me accountability. I could have blamed others when things didn't go my way, but I chose to correct every micro and grave mistake. Mistakes are far better than regret. If I didn't try, I'd be haunted by what-ifs and missed opportunities. Taking risks might lead to errors, but at least I would know I gave it my all. So, make mistakes and never look back!

But here's the plot twist:

It's easy to feel unfortunate when things don't go as planned. My confidence took a hit. I managed to score in the 60s and 70s in my other subjects, but in English—the one where I wanted to shine—I ended up with just 49. It was a mark I never imagined I would get, especially in my favorite subject. Ironically, I scored 92 in Geography, a subject I had little interest in. Those numbers felt meaningless to me like they were mocking my efforts. I felt as if God was testing my determination, patience, and self-belief.

If only I had managed my time better, I thought I would have been happier. Instead, I carried a pain that was hard to explain to anyone. Everyone around me had their opinions and advice, but no one understood how much that English mark affected me.

With no other choice, I decided to take an improvement exam the following year. In the meantime, I enrolled in a B.A. program that I had zero interest in, just biding my time until I could retake my English exam. During that time, I practiced diligently to improve my time management skills. Eventually, I dropped out in my second year of college after finally achieving 81% in English.

But that wasn't the end of the story. The following year, university cutoffs soared higher than the last year, and I didn't qualify for the colleges I had hoped for. Left with no other options, I pursued my education through an open university, ensuring I wouldn't regret my decision later on.

Looking back, I've come to understand that preparation and confidence are vital, as is the ability to manage my time and emotions effectively. While it was a significant setback, it underscored the importance of staying calm and focused, regardless of how prepared or excited I might be. It was a hard lesson to learn, but it ultimately motivated me to take charge of my own journey.

"Own your choices and steer your own journey."

That journey taught me more than just realized academic lessons; it instilled a sense of accountability in me. I could have easily blamed others when things didn't go my way rather than focused on addressing every small and significant mistake I made. I realized that mistakes are far more valuable than regret. If I had chosen to dwell on my failures, I would have been haunted by what-ifs and lost opportunities. Taking risks might lead to errors, but at least I could say I gave it my best shot.

"Trying today is better than regretting tomorrow."

• 7 •

CHAPTER THREE

Regret Sucks!

"We need to realize that neither the government nor corporations will fix our problems. Instead of waiting for solutions, start loocenternward and take control of your own path."

In India, many parents dream of seeing their cfirstren become engineers or doctors or secure government jobs. These careers are viewed as golden tickets to a bright and stable future. In this pursuit, the ideals of gender equality often get sidelined. A government job, in particular, is seen as a safety net—offering not only financial security but also a sense of self that can withstand the scrutiny and taunts of relatives. This societal pressure shapes the aspirations of countless families, overshadowing the unique talents and passions of the next generation.

Government jobs may give everything, but that doesn't mean it is everything for everyone.

Before aiming for ambitious goals, many students prepare for a challenging journey, equipping themselves with knowledge and determination. However, not everyone has the innate skills to make money or the dream to become a doctor or succeed in the UPSC exam. This raises an important question: why do so many parents push their children toward these conventional careers? While some are fortunate enough to pursue their passions as artists, designers, or editors, many find themselves trapped in traditional roles, losing sight of what truly makes them happy. It's essential to recognize that success takes many forms, and nurturing each individual's unique interests is vital for a fulfilling life.

If you were to ask me what defines an artist or anyone who pursues their dreams, I would say it's someone who is never tired, never satisfied, and never give up easily and early.

Many feel stuck in traditional career paths, losing sight of what truly brings them joy. It's essential to recognize that success can take many forms, and it's crucial to support each individual's unique interests.

Those who don't prioritize meeting societal expectations often find themselves experiencing true freedom.

When you're passionate about what you do, work feels less like a chore and more like a joy. When you love what you do, you naturally aim to improve regularly. Those who truly enjoy their work aren't driven by money; they're committed to perfecting their craft, which is worth far more. While others feel trapped in careers chosen for them, spending years trying to meet expectations that may not align with their dreams. They toil away, often without anyone asking what they truly want. The relentless pursuit of these goals, regardless of the number of attempts, can lead to a harsh judgment. Whether you try five, eight, or ten times, you are immediately seen as a failure once you fail. It's only later, in quiet moments of reflection, that many realize the cost of living under the shadow of societal expectations:

"Had I not been afraid of imaginary barriers all my life, God knows how well I would have lived; he knows how proudly I would have died."

Parents' intentions are undeniably pure, rooted in love and a desire for their children's success. But the pressure starts early, in the hallowed halls of schools because real life is not taught in the classroom. In India, education often shifts focus from authentic learning and personal growth to merely scoring high marks and making a good income. This emphasizes judgment, comparison, and self-doubt that can ruin the entire game of living life in what everyone deserves.

My parents encouraged me to take government exams. So, I spent two years preparing for this because I didn't want to carry the burden of regret in the future. They envisioned a future filled with self-respect and stability, not even realizing that the path they chose might not be the one I wanted to walk. Yet, in their eyes, this was the sole route to a successful life—a narrative repeated across countless households, shapes the destinies of many, for better or worse.

Imagine a world where children are encouraged to explore their true passions without fear of judgment where success is measured not by the letters after your name but by the fulfillment in your heart. It's like a slow-acting poison—not one that ends life, but one that lingers, making you feel its sting every day.

Regret! Ladies and Gentlemen,

Regret isn't just a fleeting emotion; it's the haunting echo of moments we let slip through our fingers. It's the time we had, the people we could have connected with, the emotions we held back, and the dreams we cherished—all those first experiences that faded away because we hesitated, paralyzed by the fear of judgment from others.

While those wounds may heal over time, how do we move past the regret that clings to us like an unwelcome shadow?

When you allow precious moments to pass because of what strangers might think, you set yourself up for lasting trouble. Even decades later, at 40 or 50, the pain of missed opportunities can feel just as fresh as the day they slipped away.

It's almost like a nightmare, isn't it? "Choose to earn, and you lose nothing."

So, I urge you to break free from the monotony of your daily routine. Step out of your comfort zone, do something bold, and embrace life with open arms. One day, you'll look back and say with pride, "I opened my heart and lived fully. I am blessed."

With my pencil hovering over the page, I was ready to capture the story of my life—a life lived without regrets.

Let go of societal expectations; remember that many people are still figuring out who they are and where they're headed. It's time to chart your own path.

With my pencil hovering over the page, I was ready to capture the story of my life, a life without regrets.

Break free from societal advice because many people are still figuring out who they are and where they're headed.

While many of my school friends had clear goals—becoming doctors or engineers, or something big—who aimed for above 98% to get into top colleges, I was still finding my way. Maths was never my strong suit, but English fascinated me. I was captivated by the rhythm of rhyming poems. I often experienced a sense of rhythm and musicality that evoked a range of emotions. Reading rhymes created a pleasing sound and made the language feel more playful and accessible. I felt joy or nostalgia, as the familiar patterns transported me back to childhood or fond memories. Also, the lessons woven into the endings of each story kept me intrigued and wanting more.

After school, everything took a different turn. We've all experienced that pivotal moment in our lives—the point where childhood ends, and the future begins to unfold with new and uncharted paths where everyone has to make their own decisions. Many voices may try to sway or distract you, but when your heart and mind align, it's a sign to move forward.

The school was a world of its own—filled with laughter, friendship, and a sense of unity that made every challenge manageable. In our class of thirty students, we were more than just classmates; we were a team. Whenever our teacher assigned homework, we tackled it as a united team, from every quiz to the terrible, e-board exams.

In every group of five, there was always that one friend who did the assignments for everyone. If someone excelled in one or two subjects, they became our unofficial tutor. My brother, for instance, was an expert in Maths. Whenever I faced tricky problems, he was always there to help me, especially during tests and exams. Apart from this session, we never forgot the fun we had, like pulling each other's legs over silly mistakes, mimicking our class teacher's unique quirks, and eagerly counting down the minutes until the lunch bell rang, especially if you brought something special in your tiffin box. Those moments of laughter and mischief make our school days truly memorable.

But when school finally ended, the unity that had been our strength began to wane.

Life moved on, and everyone got caught up in their own routines. We grew up, leaving behind the innocent child that once resided in our hearts. No longer were we a tight-knit group; we had to carve our own paths, make our own choices, and face the future as individuals.

Reflecting on those school days brings a mix of nostalgia and longing. They remind me of simpler times when the future felt like a distant dream. Yet, those memories also equipped me for what lay ahead. The friendships we formed, the lessons we learned together, and the sense of unity still resonate with me.

We had to choose our paths individually, each shaped by advice and suggestions. My parents wanted me to get a government job, believing it was the best and safest option for me. My friends, on the other hand, encouraged me to try everything they thought would lead to the right place. They were right. Friends are always there for you, ready to support you without expecting anything in return. They never hesitate to offer advice, especially when times are tough, even if it doesn't always make perfect sense. Meanwhile, others had thousands of reasons to drag me down, constantly comparing me to "Sharma ji's son or daughter" who always seemed to excel effortlessly.

The world is filled with competitors, before being humans, we need to believe in our inner voice rather than outer noises.

Caught in a whirlwind of advice and expectations, I often smiled and nodded, pretending to accept everyone else's plans, all the while I trusted my own instincts.

In the end, I decided to enroll in English Honors at college. It wasn't easy to justify this choice to those around me, but I took the time to explain why it mattered so much to me.

In the meantime, I was taking classes for the competitive exams in Laxmi Nagar because my parents wanted me to try my hand at government exams. They never forced me into anything but encouraged me to explore my options, for which I'm always thankful. I spent two years immersed in preparation for these exams. Unfortunately, I didn't achieve the results my parents had hoped for.

Although, stepping out of my comfort zone opened a whole new world. I met incredible people, discovered exciting new things, and, most importantly, found two true friends—Dimple and Deepali—in that bustling place. The very first time we met was in Laxmi Nagar, where we used to attend classes for government exams and practice for a Stenography course. Yes! You've guessed it right: like many students who tried their luck for the first time in a few years, we were among them.

Our first meeting was in Laxmi Nagar, where we attended classes at the Mahendra Institute for competitive exams and stenography and we used to take classes there. Like many students who once tried their luck for the first few years of their lives, we were one of them. Our friendship stories soon became the talk of the town, spreading from our coaching center to the local samosa shop down the street. It was all because of Dimple's infectious nature that still creates a picture in my mind.

The bustling streets of Laxmi Nagar, filled with lively conversations and the hum of everyday life, bring back vivid memories of the time I spent there. Though the competitive exams didn't go as I had hoped, the experience proved to be valuable. It taught me important lessons and helped me build connections that would stay with me for years to come.

Deepali, Dimple, and I have been inseparable for seven years. We are like three peas in a pod, an unbreakable bond. Our friendship is a treasure chest overflowing with memories, each moment together a cherished gem.

In our group, there's always that one person who keeps us grounded, and for us, it's Deepali. She's the one we rely on—the voice of reason who knows just what to say at the right moment. With a spare hair tie, a comb, and a water bottle always in her bag, she's prepared for anything. Plus, she's the surprise queen, often showing up with our favorite snacks packed in a little tiffin, ready to brighten our day.

Then there's Dimple, the life of the party. Her jokes, no matter how cheesy, always manage to bring a smile to our faces. With a grin that could light up any room, she finds humor in even the toughest situations, reminding us how a good laugh can lift our spirits and ease our worries.

After finishing my classes, I decided to start teaching for two main reasons. First, I wanted to strengthen my foundation and make my learning process more interesting through daily exchanges of ideas with my students. This interaction was incredibly stimulating. Second, I needed some extra income to cover personal expenses. But honestly, the money felt like a bonus when you love what you do.

I began my teaching journey with just four students, and to my surprise, within three months, it expanded into four full batches. During this time, I realized that when you have nothing to lose, it's a perfect opportunity to turn your hobby into something meaningful. So, I embraced that chance. Things changed quickly. My advice? Don't miss your moment—give it your all when it comes.

Every evening, after returning home around 6 PM, I dedicated my time to teaching English to students of 10th to 12th class and shared insights and techniques I had gathered from my schooling, hoping to help them navigate their educational journeys.

This raised some important questions for me: Why did I choose teaching? What made it so significant in my life? What were my goals? And what inspired me to take on this role? These reflections guided me through my journey and helped me find a sense of purpose.

While teachers played an essential role in our education. I still remember the dedicated teachers at my school who worked tirelessly to cover the syllabus. However, I noticed some gaps in their approach. They often rushed through chapters, assuming we understood everything right away. This left many of us struggling with key concepts and challenging vocabulary. It quickly became apparent that we needed more interactive support and a thorough exploration of each topic.

Picture this: sitting in a packed classroom while the teacher reads aloud, and you're trying to keep pace with the material. For some students, like me, catching up on crucial details or grappling with complex ideas was often a challenge. We needed more opportunities to ask questions, discuss our thoughts, and clarify confusing points. Understanding involves more than just listening; it requires analyzing and simplifying all the important concepts through meaningful interaction or discussion.

Interactive sessions, where we could pause for discussion and ask questions, would have increased the curiosity of learning. Learning isn't just about absorbing information; it's about questioning, processing, and doing it in your own unique way.

This realization highlighted a missing element in our education: deeper engagement and support can make the learning process more effective.

We all aspire to educate ourselves and improve our quality of life by adopting new habits or skills. However, it's crucial to focus on the areas that need change, whether personally or financially. I realized that simply reading through a chapter or even an entire book wasn't sufficient; this approach felt monotonous and uninspiring. Engaging with the material in a more dynamic way would have enriched our learning experience and better prepared us for the future. So, I decided to shake things up. Instead of relying on traditional methods, I got my students involved by asking questions, participating in discussions, and working on exercises together during the last 15 minutes of class. I shifted the focus from passive listening to active engagement, and this new approach made a noticeable difference.

I didn't have any fancy tricks up my sleeve, but I had a simple goal: to make learning easier for students in their schools so they don't have silly reasons to fear failure. My approach was straightforward—I encouraged students to relate every lesson to their lives. The more they connected the stories to their everyday experiences, the better they understood them. If you love what you do personally and professionally, you're fortunate.

Surprisingly, everything went well.

I maintained this routine for two years. Even though I was young, I began to feel more self-sufficient and energized, especially as I witnessed the positive changes in my students. At the same time, I was also preparing for my own exams. Yet, I felt happy but not satisfied. We all remember the thrill of our first paycheck.

You got this! The feeling of independence is completely different. Here's the secret I am going to reveal that might open awake you:

Does being independent truly make you happy? Does it give you the freedom you've always craved? Can it shield you from every mental challenge? Will it help you fulfill all your desires? The questions may seem endless, but the answer remains the same, "Yes."

Even if we achieve financial independence, can we honestly say we're free when it comes to our mental and physical well-being?

If true independence means freedom, why don't we take the time to prioritize ourselves? At the end of the day, we all strive for the same thing—happiness. So, if independence is meant to make us happier. Then, why do we still feel weighed down by our own struggles?

The issue often lies with time constraints and societal pressures. We spend about one-third of our time working for others and another one-sixth in commuting. If we can't allocate time for self-education, skill development, and nurturing our inner selves, can we honestly call that freedom?

Imagine this: you might have a large sum of money in your bank account. Still, you're working just to meet societal expectations. Are you truly free, or do you call yourself independent?

Society always criticizes you, no matter what you do whether it's about your career choices, your marital status after 30, or your fitness level. In reality, we aren't fully independent until we make time for our well-being, health, and peace of mind. True independence means handling these areas well and knowing what it means for our lives.

Freedom(n): to ask nothing. Expect nothing. To depend on nothing.- AYN RAND

In early 2020, a global storm hit—COVID-19. The pandemic was the most challenging crisis, dramatically altering daily life. While some people found comfort in spending time with family, exploring hobbies, or enjoying remote work, others struggled with isolation, financial issues, and the loss of loved ones.

I felt especially trapped and confused as I approached the final semester of my graduate studies. With my exams postponed for a year and the surge in COVID cases causing schools, universities, and offices to close, uncertainty was everywhere, leaving everyone in limbo.

At 2 a.m., others slept with dim hopes for the next few days while I was awake, staring at the ceiling. Many terrible thoughts hovered over my head. I picked up my phone and called Dimple. I was so frustrated this time when her phone was switched off for the last three days.

No texts, no calls—her mother wasn't answering either. I felt a knot of worry tighten in my stomach; I hoped everything was okay. Just as I lay down, my phone buzzed, jolting me upright.

"No way!" I thought, almost hesitating to answer. Everything felt so overwhelming, and I wasn't ready to deal with any more bad news. But as I glanced at the screen, I saw Deepali's name. My heart pounded even harder.

"Hello?" I answered, immediately detecting a tremor in her voice. It was clear she was upset, and my concern deepened. I pressed her to tell me what was wrong, and after a moment of hesitation, she finally broke down.

"Aashi... Dimple..."

"What's wrong? Is she okay?" My stomach dropped as I sensed her struggle to find the words.

"Her phone was off for five days," Deepali stammered. Then, with a shaky breath, she delivered the unimaginable news: "Dimple is no more. She will never come back."

The weight of those words hung in the air, leaving me speechless. It felt like a punch to the gut. I could hardly breathe as we both wept on the phone, sharing a pain that was too profound to comprehend. Deepali assured me we would visit Dimple's family to understand what had happened, but the shock felt unreal, especially since I had seen her just days before.

After that night, my life crumbled like a house of cards. I wasn't prepared for this; no one is ever ready for such a loss. I found myself wishing I had reached out more, or that I had simply been a better friend. It was a stark reminder that life is fragile, and we often take those we love for granted.

We often overlook the small things, from tears over a lost pencil to smiles after losing loved ones. These moments are part of life's journey, shaping us in ways we might not always notice.

In the aftermath, all I was left with was regret. I should have made more of an effort to connect with Dimple. I wished for just one last chance to see her. If only someone had warned me, I could have taken more time to appreciate our friendship. The slow burn of regret felt more agonizing than any immediate heartbreak. It made me realize that it's the things left unsaid and undone that hurt the most.

I had always been the sensitive one, depending on others for support. I trusted too easily and had never truly faced the pain of loss until that moment. The people I relied on seemed to vanish when I needed them most. Feeling unprepared for life's harsh realities, I resolved to learn from this experience and be better prepared for whatever lay ahead.

True growth begins when you accept who you are—embracing both your strengths and weaknesses. I started to recognize the small things that brought clarity and meaning to my life. Gradually, I started to understand the little things that made sense to me.

CHAPTER FOUR

You Are The Main Character Of Your Life

What role would you play if today was the first scene in your life's movie? With so much ahead of you, you still have time to make changes, to rewrite your story, and to become the hero of your own life.

In 2020, as COVID-19 ravaged the world, people were caught in a desperate struggle for survival. Hospitals ran out of essential supplies like oxygen, and families searched endlessly for medical help, often coming up empty-handed. Funeral services couldn't keep up with the sheer number of losses, and by the end of the year, sorrow was everywhere. It wasn't just a year of isolation—it was a year of unimaginable loss.

Even after a year, the world still felt trapped. Stuck at home, we faced nights that seemed never-ending. One night, I found myself lying in bed, staring at the ceiling, unable to quiet the thoughts racing through my mind.

"How could I even think about pursuing a master's without finishing my degree? What if I failed?" The weight of not having a backup plan started to pull me under, and soon, I found myself spiraling into depression. I came to realize that putting all my hope into one goal without a safety net was a massive mistake. Becoming a lecturer felt like a fading dream, and the job market—even for minimum-wage roles—seemed out of reach without the right skills.

That fear became a turning point. I had to shift my thinking, adapt, and focus on what I could control. Life isn't about having all the answers from the start; it's about finding the way through uncertainty.

Lost and unsure of who I really was, I grappled with questions that kept me up at night: What truly makes me happy? What am I passionate about? What drives me? And more importantly, what gives my life meaning?

During those tough days, tears often visited me at night. I longed for the support of those who once stood by me, but their absence made me feel utterly hopeless. But here's the thing—once you face those bitter truths, nothing stays the same. I learned that the hard way.

Deep down, no matter how broken you feel inside, no one else can see it, fix it, or heal it. The responsibility is solely yours. And once I grasped that reality, my expectations of others dropped to almost nothing.

In the midst of the chaos, a stark realization hit me: I had overlooked the most important person in my life—myself. I had spent so much time trying to live up to others' expectations and keep them happy that I forgot to figure out what made me happy. In the rush to please everyone, I lost sight of who I really was.

Questions matter. So, I started asking myself: What's an alternative now? What can I do next? Is it worth staying stuck in the past, or is it time to move ahead? It was a very conceivable solution to come out of any tough situation. I began auditing myself until I found all the solutions to these questions, and this simple habit made a world of difference.

This mindset shift made all the difference. I started to regularly reflect on my life, looking for answers within myself. That simple habit was the turning point, and slowly, it brought clarity and strength to face whatever came next.

You are the only one who can motivate and encourage yourself to be a CANDOR, not a PRETENDER.

I stumbled upon a simple yet life-altering routine that helped me confront my toughest questions. Every night after dinner, I'd head up to the terrace for just ten minutes of talking to myself. At first, it felt strange—awkward even—but I stuck with it. A week later, that short reflection time turned into an hour-long walk, filled with positive self-talk. Gradually, I realized that talking to myself wasn't crazy; it was clarity. I used those moments to review my day, plan for tomorrow, and reflect on any lessons learned. Surprisingly, those quiet conversations with myself revealed parts of me I didn't even know existed, and with each passing day, I felt myself growing into a better version of who I was.

Soon, this routine became an essential part of my life. I began to notice something profound: I no longer needed validation from others because I was beginning to truly understand and support myself. The more I talked to myself, the more clarity I gained, and it helped me figure out who I was and what I wanted. My real journey toward self-awareness began when I stopped hiding behind excuses and fully embraced who I was. No more pretending—this new honesty with myself shifted everything.

When things didn't go as planned, I'd write down my thoughts and ask myself tough, uncomfortable questions. It felt like unloading a heavy burden off my shoulders—though it wasn't easy. It took years of practice to confront uncomfortable truths, but over time, I stopped letting others' opinions hurt or weaken me. This process turned into my biggest source of motivation. What started as a strange habit became a powerful tool for self-discovery and changing how I thought about my life.

I turned to motivational videos for help, especially Sandeep Maheshwari's sessions. His words resonated deeply with my struggles, and for 25 to 30 minutes, his insights gave me a sense of hope. But then, the next day, the heaviness returned. That's when I realized—no motivational video could change my life if I didn't know what steps to take next. Real change had to come from within.

But then, the next day, the heaviness returned. That's when I realized—no motivational video could change my life if I didn't know what steps to take next. Real change had to come from within.

When you have a meaningful purpose, motivation becomes unnecessary.

Here's the crux of it: our biggest fear is often confronting the truths we'd rather ignore. Pleasure and motivation might give us temporary relief letting us sidestep uncomfortable realities. This cycle kept repeating. Even though I heard the right advice, it never truly resonated. I grew frustrated and resentful, especially when others didn't understand despite my efforts to explain. I realized that inspirational videos are like painkillers—they offer short-term relief but don't address the root problems. Real progress begins when you confront the situation and tackle it practically and instantly. When you start seeing life as it really is, everything becomes clearer and easier.

These experiences showed me that self-reflection and genuine connections are more valuable than just listening to motivational words. We must confront our fears and apply what we've learned. This is how we move past quick fixes and find lasting strength and positivity.

Choices can simplify tough situations. You may not always control your changing feelings or thoughts, but you can decide how to respond. Don't let these challenges drain your energy.

Understanding this was like a lightbulb moment for me. I began setting aside time each day for self-reflection and journaling my thoughts and fears in detail. I reached out to friends and family, seeking genuine connections and conversations. Slowly, I began to see changes. It wasn't easy, and there were days when I fell back into old habits, but the progress was undeniable.

There are moments in life when you realize that true change starts from within. It's not about finding temporary motivation from the success stories of others. It's about exploring your own truths and experiences while surrounding yourself with a support system that genuinely understands and encourages you.

One day, I stumbled upon a video of a public figure entrepreneur speaking about "Not caring about what others think" on YouTube.

His 52-minute speech resonated deeply with me and I couldn't wait to implement his insights into my life. I've been following him for the past five years, and what sets him apart is his courage to address the hard truths about life to the world and that has saved and transformed millions of lives.

Day by day, his words started to shape my life. Surprisingly, the toughest lessons I learned from him led me to self-awareness and this was truly a game-changer for me. However, the tale of sorrow ends here. The tears had dried up, and I thought I had reached a plateau when suddenly, one simple yet powerful moment entered and changed the entire direction of my life.

Everything falls into place when you're true to yourself.

CHAPTER FIVE

The Game of "Why Not?"

"Never underestimate yourself, especially in the toughest moments. God has a greater plan for you, and your challenges today will reveal your true purpose tomorrow." If you're facing turbulence or pressure, it's probably because you're on the rise. There will be moments when you give your everything, only to be met with cynicism or skepticism. Don't let that crush you—let it drive you. In a world where anyone can say anything about you at any time you can't stop them from doing this. But remember this:

you have every right to prove them wrong.

Everything happens for a reason, and we all must discover how. Why did I choose English Honors and spend a year that felt wasted? I never intended to pursue a career in writing. Everything seems ordinary until you uncover the hidden magic within it.

Every night, I stayed up late preparing for a final exam that hadn't even been announced yet. Then, out of nowhere, I came across an app I had never heard of—Quora. It was a platform where you could gain knowledge, share insights, and get quality answers—at least, that's what Google claimed when I searched for it.

I remember clearly the day I installed the app on my phone. The first answer that popped up was from a guy named Divyansh Mundra. Out of curiosity, I checked his profile and discovered he was a bestselling author, an avid reader, and a talented storyteller. Instantly, I was hooked. All the worries and doubts I had earlier seemed to vanish. When you come across something that truly resonates with who you are—your thoughts, your personality—you can't help but dive in, ignoring the obstacles and setbacks that might come your way.

The question was about his life and career. As I went through his answers, something sparked within me. It lit a fire that had been quietly smoldering in the back of my mind. It wasn't about perfect grammar or fancy words—two things I wasn't particularly familiar with at the time. What really caught my attention was the way he unapologetically shared his thoughts. His confidence and honesty were magnetic, and I suddenly felt like I could do the same.

From that moment on, I set out to capture that boldness in my own writing. But as I dove into my journey, I quickly learned a hard truth: opening up is tough. It takes courage to be real with yourself and even more to share that with others. I realized that authenticity isn't about striving for perfection but about owning every part of who you are, including the flaws.

Great ideas rarely come easy, but I found that the more I wrote, the more my ideas began to flow. That first spark led me to create posts daily, and with each one, I felt a deep sense of fulfillment. But I also learned that having a brilliant idea doesn't always mean the end result will be brilliant. In fact, sometimes, ideas get in the way of the writing itself. One of the first lessons for any new writer is understanding that we all start as readers. We don't just pick up books to see words—we do it to be moved by the stories within that reminds us we are not alone.

Initially, I made plenty of mistakes and didn't receive much engagement. I faced negative comments and felt uncertain about sharing my writing on other social media platforms. So, what did I do? I chose to ignore the negativity and kept writing. I realized that it wasn't about achieving perfection; it was about making progress, which is exactly what I needed at that time.

Following Divyansh wasn't about trying to become a replica of him; I wanted to absorb everything I could about writing. Then, I asked myself, "If he can do this, why can't I?" That question sparked something within me, and that night marked a turning point. I understood that my journey had begun, and I was ready to embrace it fully.

When you're at your lowest, the little things begin to matter more. It's understanding that even small steps help you bounce back from rock bottom, and that's what builds resilience. I had no backup plan, no formal skills, and no experience. Writing was the only thing that felt natural to me, something that came straight from my core. It became my nightly escape. I'd always dreamt of becoming a lecturer, but the pandemic turned that dream upside down. Life, I learned, isn't about doing what we love—it's about finding what's right for us.

Call it fate or luck, but writing became a force I was determined to master. It gave me a way to release emotions I had buried deep inside—especially the grief of losing a friend and the regret surrounding my career decisions.

Quora turned into a safe space where I could openly discuss the challenges I was going through. Trusting my gut, I began writing down my thoughts and sharing them with the world. It became a powerful tool for expressing my experiences and connecting with others who might be going through the same struggles. And oh, how I love writing by hand. There's something deeply satisfying about putting pen to paper, capturing raw thoughts about life's truths and human nature's complexities. When I look at those messy, overflowing pages of ideas, stories, and experiences, I feel a deep sense of fulfillment.

When one dream fades, another emerges.

Writing was never my childhood dream, nor did I have a natural talent for it. I wasn't one of those avid readers, and I didn't come from a family where writing was emphasized. Even when I began writing, there was no one to guide me—no advice, no direction. But despite that, hope and a sense of happiness were what filled me when I made it a habit.

On April 7, 2020, at 4 a.m., I posted my first-ever answer on Quora about my dear friend Dimple. To my surprise, responses began trickling in that very day. It was just a small step—posting that first answer. The grammar was a mess, the writing style was far from polished, but I hit "publish" anyway. And despite all its flaws, that post gave me a sense of fulfillment, excitement, and the drive to keep going. Who cared if there wasn't much engagement or if I wasn't instantly on top of the world? I didn't let it stop me. I made it a point to post one answer every single day.

At first, expressing myself was difficult, and it took time to find my voice. But I kept at it. For the next five years, I spent countless nights honing my craft, always aiming higher. My desire to write for a larger platform grew as I found purpose in the process. I continued posting on Quora, embracing the criticism and learning from my mistakes. In 2020, even though my writing wasn't perfect, I realized how much I loved the process.

Answering questions, especially around mental health, opened my eyes to how everyone has their own battles. At times, I'd wonder why anyone would care about my thoughts or take the time to read what I had to say. I had to push past those doubts and realize the value in my voice.

People don't always seem indifferent because they don't care; most are quietly fighting their own battles. There were days when I felt completely lost, and nights when everything felt off. The funny thing is, whenever I found myself stuck, I'd sit down and write out every last detail until a solution appeared. Once I had things figured out, I'd let it go. That's been my way of working through life—documenting the struggles and sharing what I've learned on social media, reminding others that they're not alone. Writing became a form of therapy for me, turning problems that once felt heavy into things I could easily release.

I've come to realize that only a few are willing to sacrifice something meaningful to gain something greater. These are the people who aren't broken by failure, loss, or the endless struggle to rise again. Sometimes, it's hope that keeps them going. For me, writing became that source of hope and direction, something that gave meaning to the chaos.

I quickly learned to brush off the negativity from people who seem to exist just to tear others down. But here's the funny part—after posting my first piece, I spent the next day Googling questions like, "What is writing?" "How does it work?" and "What's the structure?" You might laugh, but that's how I started—by asking the most basic questions. It's easy to feel insecure when you're at the very beginning, especially when it feels like everyone else has already figured it out.

Inspired by Divyansh, I slowly carved out my own writing path. Reading other writers not only made me want to write more, but it sharpened my awareness of the world around me. I began to see how essential listening and observing were to improving my writing. The more I observed, the more I could infuse my work with meaning, making it feel real and relatable for others.

From the very start of my writing journey, there was one person who consistently guided me. No matter how basic my questions were, he always had an answer. Whether it was about staying motivated or something as abstract as, "What exactly is writer's block?", he'd always talk me through it. He wasn't just a mentor—he was an incredible storyteller, a hilarious guy, and felt more like a brother. One piece of advice he repeated countless times was, One piece of advice he repeated countless times was, "There shouldn't be a gap between what you think and what the reader understands." If your writing doesn't match your thoughts, the message gets lost.

In the months that followed, my posts barely got any views, and I received harsh comments because my words just didn't connect with people. After countless attempts, I realized that no one cared about my content or flashy language. If my writing wasn't structured or clear, it was simply overlooked.

I've always been driven by curiosity and a desire for change. I was constantly on the lookout for fresh and unique ideas. So, despite honing my writing skills, I leaped and signed up for fundamental courses on trusted platforms like Google, Udemy, and Internshala. In addition, I reached out to friends who were skilled writers, asking for their honest feedback and advice. With a steadfast routine, I dedicated myself during the quiet hours, either mornings or nights, to self-learning and practice and just tried to stay consistent in the pursuit of improvement.

In March 2022, amidst everything I had going on, I received an email from my college—final exams were scheduled. With just two months to prepare for the exam, I had no choice but to set everything else aside and focus on my studies. After a year and a half, the thought of cracking open the books and facing that final exam felt daunting—it was a struggle to muster up the motivation. But I tried as hard as I could in my final exams. I used to be proud of never failing, always saying I had never stumbled or faced defeat. But the truth is, you don't really understand how hard it is until you experience it yourself.

Four months later.

It was just an ordinary evening until my phone buzzed. It was a friend from college, and I could hear the urgency in his voice as he mentioned the results were out. My stomach tightened as I quickly opened the college website. I entered my roll number and hit 'enter.' My eyes widened in disbelief as I saw the screen. I had failed one subject. The shock hit me hard, leaving me confused and unsure of what had gone wrong.

I went straight to my elder brother, who's always been my rock through every challenge. He's the one who cheers me on, even when others doubt me. I was nearly breathless as I tried to explain what happened, but he just smiled and laughed, taking it all in stride as if it didn't bother him.

"First failures always sting," he reassured me. With genuine empathy, he began sharing his own experiences with failure, recounting stories from his college days and moments from his professional life. Hearing his examples made it easier to understand my situation. Through his experiences, I realized I wasn't alone in facing setbacks; failure is a crucial part of growth.

""Have you talked to your father?" he asked, his voice steady as I processed his advice.

I hesitated, finally breaking the silence. "Not yet."

I hadn't shared my exam results with anyone yet; I wanted to sort things out first. I wasn't afraid of failing, but I genuinely believed I had done well on the paper. For now, I chose to keep it to myself, knowing that more information might come from the college soon. A few days later, I learned that many other students had struggled with their exams during COVID-19 as well. This encouraged me to give it another try and continue pursuing my degree because it truly mattered to me.

A few months later, I prepared to retake the same exam I had previously failed. This time, I was determined to do more than just pass; I wanted to ensure I wouldn't fail again. Everything aligned just as I had hoped, and eventually, it all fell into place.

Whatever happens in your life means something, even if you are too small to understand 'Why'.

CHAPTER SIX

A Stem Of Fear "Comfort Zone"

"Battle Scars Are Attractive"

Nothing was really working in my favor. Life wasn't exactly a smooth ride, and every step I took seemed to come with its own set of challenges, just like anyone else. But here's the thing:

I started looking at each obstacle as an opportunity. That shift in perspective helped me push through whatever life threw my way. I've grown to love challenges—they ground me and keep me connected to what's truly important. I've come to realize that the first attempt at anything always feels tough or discouraging, but once you face it, it doesn't seem as intimidating anymore.

There's a certain satisfaction in confronting difficulties head-on, in seeing people's true nature when their facades slip away. Life is like a complicated friend—sometimes it feels like an ally, other times like an adversary. But more often than not, it's that unpredictable companion that throws surprises your way, leaving you to deal with them as best you can.

As I navigated life's ups and downs, I felt both joy and frustration. But in the end, I realized that life didn't really change; it was just presenting me with new tests. Life is messy, beautiful, unpredictable, but always real. And what truly matters is how we face it, adapt, and keep moving forward, no matter the chaos.

Consistency became a lesson I truly absorbed for the first time. I didn't stop posting on Quora, even when I saw other writers in the community who had already hit the big numbers—millions of views—by sharing captivating fiction in genres like suspense, horror, fantasy, and poetry. Their success didn't discourage me; in fact, it fueled me. I thought, "Why not give it a shot?" So, I did. I dabbled in sketching and leaped writing suspense and thriller stories. Why? Because I had nothing to lose. Nobody knew I was trying it, so there was no fear of judgment if I failed.

At that time, I had no real understanding of how to write fiction. I didn't know how to craft a central plot or develop it. All I understood were the basics—characters and climaxes. But as I started immersing myself in stories on the platform, reading how others captured readers' attention with unexpected twists and fresh perspectives, new ideas began forming in my mind. It was as if reading their work sparked a creative energy in me that I hadn't felt before.

Surprisingly, my first 400-word story gained traction. The response was more than I expected, and it drove me to dive deeper. I began incorporating a routine of observing the world around me, drawing from everyday moments, and letting those observations shape my writing. As a result, my stories grew more engaging, attracting more readers, upvotes, and positive feedback. Little by little, I became hooked on the writing process itself.

With a clearer focus, I laid out a strategy in my notebook, and the next day, I executed it as I had planned.

I answered questions like, "Can you write a story with a twist ending?" and "What's the best advice you would give for living one life?" At the same time, I often talked about the importance of mental health and exercise, encouraging readers to prioritize both in their lives. Through all the experimentation and patience, I found myself fully absorbed in the process, eager to keep growing as a writer.

What was the major reason behind it? Everyone loves to gather health tips and techniques, but when it comes to waking up early, most struggle. It's not about following the latest trends. At some point, everyone reaches that realization—wishing they had taken their health more seriously. When I ran out of things to say, I'd always fall back on coffee—it was my favorite conversation starter. There wasn't an easy way to improve overnight, but the more I talked about health and wellness, the more I learned.

Applause to those who truly invested in themselves, building their skills without falling into the trap of "it's not for me" or "this is beyond my abilities."

"I believe it's far from over—any time you invest in yourself will never go to waste. That's something I've learned firsthand."

Even though the worst of COVID-19 had passed, the effects lingered. Many were still mourning lost loved ones, and hospitals remained filled with uncertainty and grief. Each phone call carried a sense of fear. Yet amidst the heaviness, there was resilience as people began to move forward, determined to restart their lives, step by step.

During this time, I took it upon myself to seize every opportunity. I started by crafting a resume and building a profile on various job platforms. Day by day, I sent out applications for content writing internships. I knew this was a skill I wanted to sharpen, so I applied to multiple companies.

A week later, I got my first interview call from a company. Excited but nervous, I prepared as best as I could, practicing my introduction repeatedly. Even though I didn't feel entirely ready, I told myself that facing rejection was better than not trying at all. The interview, however, didn't go well. I stumbled over my words, my confidence wavered, and my lack of knowledge became painfully clear. But I wasn't ready to give up. I stayed focused, knowing that the next opportunity could be just around the corner. What was driving me forward?

It was simple—I couldn't afford to wait until I felt completely ready. Even small wins amidst the failures showed me that continuing was worth it. I trusted my gut.

Want to hear something you might already know? Trusting your instincts gets easier when you truly believe in what you're doing.

MMy parents didn't quite get it. They'd often tell me I was wasting my time. Friends told me I wouldn't make it, no matter how much effort I put in. No one really asked what I was working on, and I never tried to explain it to them.

Then, out of nowhere, my phone rang from an unfamiliar number. I picked up, and a polite voice greeted me.

"Hello, is this Aashi?"

"Yes, speaking."

"Hi, Aashi. I'm pleased to inform you that your application for the content writing internship has been shortlisted. Would you be available for an interview on Monday at noon?"

"Oh, thank you! Yes, I'm available."

"Great! I'll schedule it for Monday at noon. Does that work for you?"

"Absolutely, that works."

"Wonderful. I'll send you a confirmation email shortly. Could you acknowledge it when you receive it?"

"Of course, I will. Thank you."

"Do you have any questions for me?"

"No, I think I'm all set. Thanks again!"

"Fantastic. We look forward to meeting you. Goodbye!"

"Goodbye."

And with that, she hung up the call.

I couldn't wait to call Deepali and share the news. She was the one person who always gave me honest feedback and shared in my excitement. We celebrated together, and it felt great to have someone who truly understood. Afterward, I told my dad. He was a bit puzzled at first, wondering how I got the opportunity. I explained that I'd been working on building a specific skill over the past few months. It took a little while, but he finally understood.

When Monday arrived, a mix of nerves and excitement churned inside me. I couldn't stop wondering—what kind of questions would they throw at me? How should I frame my answers? My mind was spinning, but one thought calmed me: even if I didn't get the job, this interview would still be a valuable experience. At least I'd learn something from it.

Just as my self-doubt was creeping in, a voice called my name, snapping me back to reality. "Aashi, please come in." I walked into the room where three people were seated, waiting for me. But, I was prepared for it.

"So, Aashi, tell us a bit about yourself."

Like most freshers, I began the interview with the usual introduction—my name, where I was from, my interests, and why I wanted to join their company. But as I spoke, my nerves got the better of me. My voice wavered, and I stumbled over my words. Sensing my discomfort, the interviewers exchanged a quick glance and gently said, "It's okay, no worries. Take your time." They wrapped up soon after, giving me a reassuring nod, as if to say, "We've all been there."

They spent about thirty minutes reviewing my performance before giving us a task to complete in 25 minutes on a specific topic. I wasn't alone—there were five more candidates with me. One interviewer collected our phones and left us to finish the task. The final decision would be based on this test. We submitted our work, and they said, "We'll call you."

At first, I was confused by what "We'll call you" truly meant. When I got home, I shared everything with my brother. He said, "If they were impressed, they would have decided immediately. Being told they'll call you later usually means you're on hold, or they might not be selecting you. I noted that the other candidates seemed more seasoned and skilled. This left me feeling uncertain, and I began preparing myself for the chance that I might not be selected. My brother told me not to wait for a call or set my hopes too high. "Stay optimistic," he said. "Take this as a learning experience, improve your weaknesses, and keep pushing forward. It's just the start, Aashi."

Three days passed, and I continued the same process of searching for jobs and improving further. I had nothing to lose, so I had to move on. Suddenly, I received a call from the company where I had interviewed.

"Hello Aashi Sharma, I am calling from this company, I let you know that you've been selected for the position of Content Writing internship.

After hearing the news, a tear glistened in my eye while a wide smile remained.

"Thank you so much! I'm excited to join this company," I couldn't fully express my happiness during the call with HR.

"When can you start?"

"I can begin on Monday."

"Perfect! I'll send you the official offer letter via email shortly. Please confirm receipt and reach out if you have any questions."

"Thank you so much!"

"We're excited to have you on board, Aashi!"

As soon as she ended the call, I rushed to my brother, wrapping my arms around him tightly as tears of joy filled my eyes. He had sensed my excitement from the moment I picked up the call but wanted to hear from me. I shared everything, and he wished me all the best as I embarked on this new chapter.

What the future held was a mystery. No one knew. People who chase better opportunities sometimes make mistakes by following others' advice.

The next Monday morning, I woke up early, buzzing with anticipation for my first day. In her usual loving way, my mother packed my lunch just like she did when I was in school. making the day feel nostalgic and surreal. Before I left, she offered me a spoonful of curd and sugar, "For good luck," her smile radiating.

I felt a whirlwind of emotions—excitement, nerves, and a hint of fear—as I prepared for my first day at work. It was a big step, and I was both thrilled and anxious. My dad shared in my feelings too. When I grabbed my bag and headed for the door, he was waiting with the car keys, ready to take me to the bus stop.

As I arrived a few minutes early on my first day, my heart raced with anticipation. My manager greeted me with a warm handshake, introducing me to the team and providing a brief overview of my role. As I settled into my desk, I noticed the girl next to me.

She was casually chewing gum and humming a song, her head bobbing with some beat only she could hear. It was as if she was in her own little world, fully engrossed in her tasks, with a natural ease that made everything look effortless. It was captivating to watch, her energy and joy were palpable.

But my attention kept drifting back to my manager, who seemed occupied with work and other teammates, barely pausing between calls and tasks. I needed to clear the doubts swirling around my head but hesitated about how to interrupt him.

Seeing my hesitation, that girl said, "What are you looking at? Need some help?"

I replied softly, "Yes, I am just waiting for him to be available so I can ask a few things"

She chuckled. "You don't have to wait. I'm right here. Ask away."

Her confidence was reassuring. "It's just a lot to take in, you know? I'm not sure where to start."

She nodded, sympathetically. "It may take some time to figure out how to write content for clients at a good pace as we all do, but give yourself time to understand the process here. You'll learn as you go. I admitted, "I've only ever written for myself before. What if I make mistakes?"

He reassured me, "That's how you'll learn and know better about this."

I smiled, feeling a bit more confident.

To ease my tension, she gave me an example of her friend who was once in the same situation and felt completely lost for a few months. However, with time and effort, her friend learned and excelled in her role.

She patiently cleared all my doubts and said, "Once you learn the basics and start writing a few paragraphs, it will no longer be difficult." Still, she politely answered all my questions, making everything seem manageable. Her encouragement and support made me feel more confident, comforting me that I could handle the challenges ahead.

At lunch, she introduced me to a few of her teammates. We gathered around a table, passing around our food and exchanging stories about our experiences. Their warm and welcoming nature helped dissolve the tension I had felt earlier, making it easy to connect and share a few laughs. By the end of the meal, I felt like I was already becoming part of the team, the camaraderie easing my nerves significantly.

And, that's how my first day wrapped up—full of unexpected support, friendly faces, and the realization that I wasn't as alone as I thought.

The usual office hours are from 10 AM to 6 PM. That day, after leaving work, it took me an hour and a half to get home. I felt exhausted and uneasy because this job wasn't part of my routine. I felt insecure because I had missed my practice and other things. Discomfort comes from stepping out of your comfort zone. My connection with the past, unease with the present, and fear of the future made me make the biggest mistakes.

As I stepped out of the office, my phone buzzed with a call from my mother.

"Have you left the office?" she asked, her voice filled with anticipation.

"Yes, Mummy. I'm heading toward the metro station now," I replied, moving through the busy street.

"How was your first day?" she asked, eager to hear about my first experience on the first day.

"It was great! Everyone was supportive, kind, and friendly. They shared the good parts of the job that made me feel better," I said, trying to convey how better I felt.

She sighed with relief. "I'm so glad to hear that. Did you manage to eat something?"

"Yes," I lied, glancing at my watch. I was running late and hadn't found a chance to grab a bite.

I quickly booked a cab from the office to the metro station, knowing I still had an hour's ride home.

The next morning, as I got ready for work, I felt completely drained. My body ached, and I struggled to shake off the sleepiness in just one day. Not many, especially my parents, were happy about the long hours and the distance. I didn't realize that taking others' opinions seriously could cost me a lot. All these reasons piled up, pushing me towards a drastic decision: quitting my job. Little did I know, I was about to make a huge mistake.

I sat down and texted a long message on my phone. The moment I hit 'send.' Within five minutes, my manager pinged me on WhatsApp, asking why I had decided to leave so abruptly. I gave him the reasons I thought were valid, but deep down, I knew I could have handled things better.

Many people stick with their jobs for years, whether it's for financial stability or gaining experience. I hadn't truly considered that. I wanted to learn and explore, but in my haste, I had given up my first job far too quickly.

This impulsive decision left a deep impression on my career, but I held onto a strong belief in myself. I knew I could keep learning, improving, and trying in different companies. This was just the beginning, and I was determined not to let one mistake define my path.

The circle of your comfort zone is too small, let's expand it until you feel good about it.

In mid-2022, I landed my second hybrid job as a content writer for a company in Jaipur. It was a time when millions were adjusting to the new normal of working from home during the lockdown. While some embraced the chance to blend work and home life, others found the transition far from easy.

Mornings no longer started with the frantic rush to catch a train or beat the traffic. Instead, they began with a peaceful cup of coffee in the kitchen, often still in pajamas. These individuals discovered a newfound balance where they could step away from their desks to play with their kids, take a walk in the evening, or even pursue hobbies that had long been on hold. The flexibility brought a sense of control and freedom, letting them shape their days around their needs and family commitments.

On the flip side, not everyone found this transition so smooth. The reality of remote work was a constant juggle for many. Reliable high-speed internet wasn't available to everyone, and technical glitches were a daily frustration. The absence of a dedicated workspace meant working from kitchen tables or crowded living rooms, often with family members sharing the same space. The line between work and home blurred, leading to longer hours and a struggle to disconnect. Parents, especially, had a hard time balancing work with homeschooling and childcare.

Amid all this, many were trying to earn enough money to support financially and feed their families. Some, like me, had nothing but sheer belief and little hope to hold onto. I kept telling myself, "I can handle this. When the opportunity comes, I'll make it work." Ultimately, it all came down to believing in yourself and pushing through.

I had a mindset—if this didn't work out, I would explore another path. Believe it or not, amazing things happen when you genuinely give it your all. That belief kept me going. With that in mind, I moved on to the second company. I learned from previous experience, determined to stick with it, no matter how challenges I faced. As I settled into my new role, I realized I was on my own—there was no team to exchange talk, no one to motivate me, and no one to make me feel better and comfortable.

I had just a few days to gather everything I needed to work from home. But I wasn't worried about it all. I borrowed a second-hand laptop and set it up on my hotspot, and there was one person I knew a tech-savvy friend would be available to help me if I ran into any problems. Now, all good to go!

As an intern, I crafted travel blogs and managed content for the company's social media platforms.

"You need to write a 600-word blog. I'm sending you an email with the details," she said, adding, "If you need any help, don't hesitate to ask." As an email hit my inbox, I wondered, 'I had never written anything that long earlier. How was I supposed to finish it in two hours?

They provided some reference websites to help me get started and mentioned a few keywords to include. So, I tried. Then, I started researching, writing, and trying to make the blog engaging with pictures, informative by using examples, and inspiring by adding value.

It took me 4 hours to finish my first blog on my first day. During that time, they called me multiple times to remind me that I was running late. Even after that, I submitted the blog at 4 in the evening. They had a lot to say about my task but they simply warned me that the next time I would avoid repeating the same mistakes.

On my second day, she asked me to write a 1000-word blog about Ladakh and sent over the instructions. Unsure how to write such a long piece, I reached out for help. "I've never written a blog this long, and I don't think I can finish it in just two hours. Can you help me figure out how to do it?" I asked. Even though I had doubts, I knew I couldn't avoid challenges as a professional.

I started with an introduction that captured the breathtaking beauty of Ladakh—the towering mountains, clear blue skies, and serene monasteries. My goal was to make readers feel like they were already there. I wrote the blog to give readers a real feel of Ladakh. It wasn't just a task; I wanted to share important and heartfelt information with the audience. I began with an introduction that painted a vivid picture of Ladakh's awe-inspiring beauty—the rugged mountains, the clear blue skies, the serene monasteries settled among the hills, and one of the most breathtaking sights in Ladakh is the cluster of stars that light up the night sky. I wanted my readers to feel like they were actually there, soaking in the view.

I love the knack of scouting and this is one of the best sources I have ever had. As I worked on each blog, I carefully chose scenic photos that captured the essence of Ladakh. Each image showcased a unique aspect of this stunning region, from the ancient stupas of Thiksey Monastery to the turquoise waters of Pangong Lake shimmering under the golden hues of the setting sun.

Alongside the visuals, I included practical advice. I shared tips on the best time to visit, what to pack, how to travel, and how to deal with high-altitude regions. And of course, I couldn't resist adding more captivating images—vibrant prayer flags fluttering in the wind to the winding roads cutting through Ladakh's stark terrain.

I didn't stop at facts and photos. I wrapped up each blog by highlighting the special moments that make a trip to the place unforgettable.

I painted pictures that made exceptional experiences for travelers — a night under a blanket of stars, the taste of traditional Ladakhi cuisine, and experiencing the warmth of the local hospitality. With each paragraph, I aimed to leave a lasting impression. And, showcasing why they deserved a top spot on anyone's travel bucket list.

Behind the scenes, I had never set foot in Ladakh, but I immersed myself in research, allowing my imagination to paint the landscapes and experiences. I spent the entire day crafting and refining the blog until I felt it was ready. The next morning, I received a call from my manager. To my surprise, she praised my writing, saying they were impressed with the vivid imagery and engaging narrative. I was over the moon, relieved that my effort had paid off.

As time went on, the work became increasingly demanding. Some days were thrilling, while others were filled with frustration. Then came a new assignment: I was tasked with creating content for a promotional poster, something completely. Through it all, I realized it's normal to feel unsure, even when you try something new or seemingly impossible. Over time, I started feeling better by pushing myself outside my comfort zone.

After I submitted my work, my manager called me, and I could hear the laughter of a few colleagues in the background. Confused and a bit hurt, I asked, "What's so funny? Did I make a mistake?" Instead of offering constructive feedback, my manager simply told me to revise the work and submit it again by the next morning before abruptly ending the call. I felt a wave of humiliation wash over me, and frustration bubbled up inside. It was hard not to take their laughter personally, making me doubt my skills and wonder if I truly belonged in this role. For the first time since starting, I cried and considered quitting this company.

So, I chose self-respect over anything and left the organization in the middle of the month.

Educate or not, nobody has the right to disrespect others.

When I started to overthink, it felt like everything was falling apart. My focus slipped away, and I lost my mental peace. It consumed my energy for almost a week, but I knew I couldn't stay stuck. I had to keep moving forward, no matter how small the steps. Even today, whenever I overthink I get over it by reminding myself:

"You're going to switch places, leave behind fleeting moments, and maybe even some people. So why overthink and act like there's only one path? Take a breath, and be mindful of where and with whom you spend your time. Protect your mental peace at any cost."

After trying in various companies, I learnt how to give interviews, communicate effectively, increase confidence, and take their feedback positively. The process was a mix of excitement and awkwardness. As a beginner eagerly applying to every job I found, I almost got scammed by companies asking for money upfront. Most of my experience was with hybrid jobs, so I didn't know the best way to handle face-to-face interviews, find the right company, or prepare for opportunities in new places. Unfortunately, I wasn't selected for any of them. Well, If you have the ability to earn, you're less worried about losing.

Tons of mistakes and thousands of failures are just the tip of the iceberg of the process. If you still love the game, you are unbeatable.

Initially, working in the corporate world wasn't easy for me. I didn't expect accolades, applause, or praise from others. So, I was prepared for the bad days, embracing the reality that I would inevitably make mistakes and learn from them.

After quitting that company, I faced 30 rejections before finally landing a job on the 31st attempt. It never felt like I was wasting my time or burning out, especially when I turned my passion into my career. I genuinely started to enjoy my work and started to become happier than before.

Life is too short for those who enjoy what they do and have, and long for those who haven't figured it out yet.

During this period, I worked as an English trainer at Mahendra Institute. I eventually left because I felt suffocated not pursuing a writing career, which turned my life around and brought me immense joy and freedom. Each rejection during those six months taught me an essential lesson that maybe I couldn't have learned anywhere else. The first rejection stung. But, it didn't break either my gut or my morale. Probably the best phrase I've ever heard is,

"You can be the sweetest peach on the tree, but there will still be people out there who don't like peaches."

knew exactly where I needed to improve and what to focus on. Instead of dwelling on rejection, I decided to concentrate on the feedback from experienced writers. When you're equipped to succeed, the fear of failure diminishes.

Get excited about showing people how right you are, and don't allow anybody to make you prove wrong.

You only have two options: keep trying to erase your fear or fallacy. Another side, lets people know how fabulous the fact is.

CHAPTER SEVEN

"Mindset"

As you have read, I've shared experiences with failures, rejections, discouragement, and losses. While these are extreme examples, it's important to remember that there are many voices and not everything is 100% true.

Mindset and self-awareness are important concepts that can reveal a lot if you take the time to really understand them.

Nobody ever took the time to teach me about life. What truly drove my growth and resilience was developing self-awareness. It began when I started investing time in myself and my craft. Through this, I got to know myself better than anyone else ever could, and that understanding gave me the power to shape the life I wanted.

No one will push you to get fit until you decide you need it for yourself. No one will remind you of how lost you are until you realize it. And, no one will show you what works best for you until you figure out what you love. The truth is, no one knows you better than you know yourself—something I realized when I hit rock bottom.

Four years ago, the thought of exercise seemed ridiculous to me. I wondered, "Who would wake up before sunrise." Health doesn't matter; I'm comfortable with how I am. Why spend so much money on a diet? Buying fruits and organic products seem like a waste.

And the time came when everyone admitted the importance of well-being since the covid happened. People began prioritizing health when they saw loved ones and others dying unexpectedly.

Taking care of health isn't just a trend—it's a wake-up call. The stress of modern life emphasizes the impact of poor health and pushes many to rethink their priorities.

I was leading a mundane life—eating poorly, staying up late, and isolating myself. I felt trapped and was close to giving up. Then something shifted. I decided to make a change by adopting a new routine: incorporating exercise and waking up early. Initially, it was quite tough. The workouts left me sore, and quitting seemed like an easy way out. But I kept going, reminding myself that this physical struggle was far better than the emotional weakness I had endured before.

What impact has exercise had on my life? It was the first step toward building a resilient mindset. Exercise has developed a level of determination in me that I didn't realize I had, along with a new sense of discipline. I've learned to work out efficiently without fancy gear. Every drop of sweat has made me stronger and more confident.

My second habit of building a mindset was to start journaling. I was solely new to writing and unaware of the powerful impact it could have. No one around me came from a writing background, and nobody suggested I try it. In this age of tapping away on phones, who wants to pick up a pen and write? I mean, who? Probably just a few people. Yet, the saying "the pen is mightier than the sword" holds truth.

Amid the chaos, everything fell into place once I started journaling freely, writing my thought process without skipping a day. The first thing I learned while writing is, to tell the truth and try to paint a vivid picture in the reader's mind. It took me years of practice to get to this point, and I am still trying to.

Whether I was writing for someone else or just for myself, the more I wrote, the better I understood how to articulate my thoughts and maintain a positive outlook—one of the toughest challenges in writing. It was like having an honest conversation with someone about transforming their life. And you know what? It started to shift my mindset and habits in a big way.

Writing wasn't just about filling pages with words; it was about helping others see and feel what I was expressing. It turned out to be more powerful than I realized. How did writing bring clarity? Simple: I wrote every day. If I felt overwhelmed, I wrote. If I wasn't in a good mood, I wrote. If I felt lost, I wrote. Whether it was a word, a sentence, or a paragraph, it never failed to lift my spirits.

No matter where you are, figuring out your own struggles is the fastest way to find your direction. How? Start figuring it out now.

Pain that generates beautiful stories inspires others, and resonates with millions is a unique force; It's not about being crazy; it's about channeling your pain, discomfort, and realizations onto paper. No one around you can lift your spirits or bring clarity the way you can for yourself. No one can imagine how different the conversations have been between you and your thoughts on a blank page.

You become exactly what you write regularly. I used to write what I needed to improve by punching the truth in my gut because I was scared of it. It took me years to be genuinely honest with myself. Why so long make it different ? Because it's not something everyone does. But the moment I started speaking my truth, and something shifted. The fear that once held me back began to fade, and with it came a new kind of courage—the courage to face life head-on, no matter what it threw at me.

I turned my vulnerability into power when I poured my mind on paper and fed my soul; magic happened. Pain, worries, and troubling issues faded slowly and diligently. Words transform—they dance with meaning. It might be difficult for me, but it's a commitment I've made for life.

Journaling requires a few minutes each day. Find a quiet spot, enjoy coffee, and write down my thoughts and feelings. This daily practice helps me understand myself better and stay productive. While some people set goals at the start of the day, I prefer to jump straight into action. Journaling, however, keeps me aligned with my core goals and helps me prioritize them. When I'm stuck and don't feel like writing, I review my old journal pages filled with raw thoughts, ideas, and techniques that helped me. They reveal different possibilities and strategies for handling any situation.

Through journaling, I create a clearer picture of myself by writing down my thoughts, ideas, and feelings. This has brought a deep sense of self-awareness into my life, allowing me to design and live according to my passions and interests. It's made me incredibly content and less swayed by outside opinions. Not everyone sees the value in journaling, so be one of the few who does. Start journaling and watch your stress melt away.

I wanted to become the strongest version of myself because I wasn't. I wanted to be more self-aware because I was selfless. I wanted to taste and try different things
Because I was timid. So, just because you are kind and
nice doesn't mean you can't be a warrior with a tenacious heart.

I wanted to become the strongest version of myself because I wasn't. I wanted to be more self-aware because I was selfless. I wanted to taste and try different things because I was timid. So, just because you are kind and nice doesn't mean you can't be a warrior with a tenacious heart.

I'm a huge fan of self-awareness and can't get enough of it. People often doubt the magic of self-discovery because they don't understand how it works. Loving yourself means being honest and proudly accepting all your flaws and imperfections.

CHAPTER EIGHT

True happiness? Zero Expectation

"Expectations can act as a subtle poison, quietly unraveling relationships, igniting conflicts, and draining your energy. They inflict pain on those who cling to them too tightly, leaving emotional wounds that can linger."

I've observed that many individuals experience loneliness or seek validation because they expect others to fulfill their needs and bring them happiness. When those expectations aren't met, it often leads to a cycle of blame, where they criticize others for failing to provide the joy or support they desired. This ongoing cycle of expectation and disappointment traps people in a state of unhappiness.

There was a time when I felt exposed and vulnerable because I dedicated so much effort to making others happy, only to feel let down when my efforts weren't reciprocated. I eventually realized that by letting go of expectations, I could turn my focus inward and offer my genuine self without any conditions. The search for understanding from others can feel like an endless journey—true fulfillment arises from within and from giving freely without anticipating anything in return.

Expectations from others can be like invisible chains, tying you to a version of yourself that isn't truly who you are. You often depend on people or things you care about. But here's the hard truth: the higher your expectations, the more you hurt yourself.

These expectations push you to fit someone else's idea of success and happiness, often leaving you frustrated and unfulfilled.

If you're inherently kind and enjoy giving, Don't let your kindness become a burden by expecting the same in return. When you don't get what you hoped for, it's easy to start blaming that person or situation for your unhappiness.

Now, imagine living without expectations from others. You'd find joy in helping people and moving forward, unburdened by the weight of unmet hopes. This shift in perspective can lead to a more fulfilling and less stressful life.

Instead of finding ways to make yourself happy or wealthy, you become so focused on pleasing others—whether it's your parents, partner, or society—that you lose sight of what you actually want. It can lead to a life filled with stress and a sense of emptiness because no matter how hard you try, it's impossible to satisfy everyone.

The cause of this is rooted in a need for validation and acceptance. We all want to be loved, respected, and seen as valuable, and sometimes that desire leads us to prioritize others' expectations over our dreams. But the harsh reality is that no matter how much you try to conform, you can never be everything to everyone. Trying to do so leaves you exhausted and vulnerable, caught in a cycle of seeking approval that's never fully satisfying.

Perhaps the most painful realization is that living up to others' expectations often means sacrificing your own authenticity. You might achieve success in their eyes, but inside, you may feel empty, as you're not living your true self. It becomes a relentless pursuit of someone else's vision. It can leave you feeling lost and unsure of your identity.

It's perfectly acceptable to have expectations, but they should be communicated, adjusted, and balanced with your own happiness. You hold the power to reshape this narrative. By protecting your happiness while spreading kindness and offering genuine value, you can create a fulfilling life that truly reflects who you are. This conscious approach can make all the difference.

CHAPTER NINE

Explore the Power of Exploration

Exploration? This force has deeply transformed who I am. By sharing my content, I've developed a deeper understanding of the world and its different perspectives.

I love the idea of a "spark of inspiration."

Many ignore this, but ideas can come from the most unexpected places—daydreaming, casual conversations, watching someone act oddly, or even when I am bored.

Ideas are everywhere, aren't they? The key is to be observant and open to them.

When you have an idea, it can spark excitement and push you to elevate your work or projects. Everything around us was once just an idea, The thrill of writing fiction for the first time, for instance. Writing fiction has greatly enriched my experience and broadened my imagination. One idea can lead to many, and those ideas have the power to transform lives or even change the world.

As Stephen King said, "As Stephen King wisely stated, "Writing isn't about making money or gaining fame; it's about enriching lives. It's about getting up, getting well, and moving forward."

People with passion can transform their lives when they explore their creativity—be it through art, writing, music, or other forms of expression. But a few brave souls ignore negative comments and low views, focusing instead on what matters. They understand that true change doesn't come from likes or comments but from consistently improving and sharing their authentic selves.

They discovered the internet was the perfect place to share what they had kept in their hearts for so long. For me, Quora was the first platform where I boldly shared my writing, something I had never revealed to anyone before.

Every social platform demands more than just flashy appearances or high-end equipment. Success comes from offering valuable content that resonates with your audience, not from superficial elements.

If you are genuine and unapologetic about their imperfections people will naturally connect with you and support your growth. I continued to write, embracing both the good and the bad as if my audience were the only one in the room. It was a deeply personal journey, and despite any doubts, I chose to share my work openly.

CHAPTER TEN

Try & Taste Everything

"We must taste things before we try them."

I have explored various paths to dedicate my life, from envisioning myself as a lecturer to discovering my passion for writing. This journey has been nothing short of magical.

In between, I tried my hand at stenography and other competitive exams for a couple of years. Then, I leapt and invested my time in learning and teaching with a different approach. But everything fell apart, and suddenly, writing took over and became my source of happiness, helping me solve all the riddles of my life. I continue to try new things in writing, and the journey continues. This is how I gain more experience. It does not limit our possibilities and experiences. Perhaps I couldn't share this story if I hadn't lived through it myself.

Perhaps I wouldn't have been able to share all this if I hadn't experienced it myself. Taste everything—Try everything—only then will you know what truly delights you."

CHAPTER ELEVEN

This part of my life, this little part of my life called "Happiness"

Why do I write every day? Is it to become a better writer, or is it something deeper?

At first, it felt impossible. But as I kept pushing forward, I started to make progress, step by step, knowing that every effort counted.

In art, there's no clear line between success and failure. Artists create until they feel satisfied. I realized that my writing wouldn't succeed unless it connected with others and resonated with their experiences. True success comes from creating work that touches people. If you're passionate about what you create and others connect

With it, you've already won.

I never thought I had a story worth sharing, one that could inspire others and show them that every journey has its turning points. My story might not have trophies or perfect endings, but it's given me something even more valuable— the freedom to be myself.Documenting my journey has been transformative. It has turned doubt into purpose and hesitation into momentum. Every story, no matter how small, has the power to touch someone.

So, what's your story? How will you make it different?

AASHI SHARMA

Epilogue

As we reach the end of "Documenting My Journey: Uncover Unheeded Realities," I find myself reflecting on the extraordinary transformation that can arise from the seemingly ordinary moments of our lives. This book began as a quest to capture the essence of personal growth, yet it has evolved into something far greater—a mirror reflecting the profound potential within each of us.

In the chapters that preceded this epilogue, we explored a tapestry of experiences that illuminate how passion can be distilled into purpose. Through the stories shared, we have witnessed how small, everyday encounters can serve as catalysts for significant change and deep self-discovery. The narratives presented are not merely personal anecdotes but universal touchstones that resonate with our collective human experience.

Writing this book has been a journey in itself—a process of uncovering, reflecting, and connecting dots that seemed disparate at first glance. I hope that these pages have inspired you to look beyond the surface of your daily routines and to find the extraordinary within the ordinary. By embracing these moments with intention and mindfulness, we open ourselves up to a richer, more authentic existence.

The journey to uncover unheeded realities is ongoing. Each of us carries the potential to transform our lives and the lives of those around us by acknowledging and acting

Upon the insights that arise from our experiences.

The stories shared here serve as a reminder that the path to personal growth is not always linear but is instead a mosaic of moments, choices, and revelations.

As you close this book, I encourage you to carry forward the lessonsand reflections that have emerged. Let them guide you in your own journey of discovery and growth. Embrace the changes that come your way, and recognize the power you hold to shape your own narrative.

Thank you for accompanying me on this exploration. It is my deepest hope that this journey has sparked a sense of possibility within you and that you are now poised to uncover and embrace the unheeded realities of your own life. Remember, the path to a more fulfilling and authentic existence begins with a single step—a step towards seeing the extraordinary in the everyday.

— Aashi Sharma